COLONIAL PEOPLE

The Colonial Cook

LAURA L. SULLIVAN

Cavendish Square

New York

Published in 2016 by Cavendish Square Publishing, LLC
243 5th Avenue, Suite 136, New York, NY 10016

Copyright © 2016 by Cavendish Square Publishing, LLC

First Edition

Website: cavendishsq.com

This publication represents the opinions and views of the author based on his or her personal experience, knowledge, and research. The information in this book serves as a general guide only. The author and publisher have used their best efforts in preparing this book and disclaim liability rising directly or indirectly from the use and application of this book.

CPSIA Compliance Information: Batch #WS15CSQ

All websites were available and accurate when this book was sent to press.

Cataloging-in-Publication Data

Sullivan, Laura L.
The colonial cook / by Laura L. Sullivan.
p. cm. — (Colonial people)
Includes index.
ISBN 978-1-50260-488-0 (hardcover) ISBN 978-1-50260-489-7 (ebook)
1. Cooking, American — History — Juvenile literature. 2. United States — History —
Colonial period, ca. 1600-1775 — Juvenile literature. I. Sullivan, Laura L., 1974-. II. Title.
TX715.K56 2016
641.5973'09'032—d23

Editorial Director: David McNamara
Editor: Andrew Coddington
Copy Editor: Cynthia Roby
Art Director: Jeff Talbot
Designer: Stephanie Flecha
Senior Production Manager: Jennifer Ryder-Talbot
Production Editor: Renni Johnson
Photo Research: J8 Media

The photographs in this book are used by permission and through the courtesy of: Art Media/Print Collector/Getty Images, cover; Gary D Ercole/Photolibrary/Getty Images, 4; Infrogmation of New Orleans/File:PensacolaWentworthAug2008Hardtack.jpg/ Wikimedia Commons, 6; North Wind Picture Archives, 9; David M. Doody/Colonial Williamsburg Foundation, 11, 14; Public Domain/ Samuel H. Kress Collection/National Gallery of Art/File:The kitchen maid by Jean-Baptiste Simeon.jpg/Wikimedia Commons, 17; Saint Louis Art Museum, Missouri, USA/Bridgeman Images, 18; Colonial Williamsburg Foundation, 21; David M. Doody/Colonial Williamsburg Foundation, 22, 27; Public domain/Uffizi Gallery/File:Giuseppe Maria Crespi - La cuoca, the kitchenmaid.jpg/Wikimedia Commons, 28; Public Domain/Henry Wigstead/File:Turnspit Dog Working.jpg/Wikimedia Commons, 30; Colonial Williamsburg Foundation, 33–34; HLPhoto/Shutterstock.com, 39; Rez-Art/iStock/Thinkstock, 40, Darryl Brooks/Shutterstock.com, 43.

Printed in the United States of America

CONTENTS

ONE

New World, New Foods

When the English first made a permanent settlement in the Americas at Jamestown Colony in Virginia in 1607, they were unprepared for survival. They were **entrepreneurs** hoping to make a profit with goods from the new world. They hoped for gold, but they'd make do with such natural resources as timber. None of them were farmers, hunters, or fishermen. What's more, they knew almost nothing about cooking.

For the first few months the **colonists** survived on food left by the ship that brought them. This was mostly **hardtack**, a dry biscuit made of flour, water, and salt that could last for years. (The oldest one today is from 1852 and still looks in good shape.) It was so hard it usually needed

Colonists did much of their cooking over a fire, whether at a kitchen hearth or at an outdoor fire, such as the one used by this reenactor.

Hardtack lasted a very long time but was tasteless and hard enough to break teeth.

Hardtack from Atlanta Area, 1862
T. T. Wentworth, Jr. Collection
The standard Army ration of bread was issued as hardtack, which was supposed to have a longer shelf life than regular bread. The crackers were often so wormy that ...ers nicknamed them "worm castles."

to be soaked or cooked before being eaten. Worms and beetles often infested the hardtack. Sometimes these insects were eaten along with the hardtack for extra nutrition.

Starving with Food All Around

Even though there was food growing, running, flying, and swimming all around them, the colonists didn't know how to make use of it. They were unfamiliar with most of the wild native plants, and didn't know how to grow crops. Most didn't even know how to hunt or fish.

Back in England, hunting and fishing were leisure activities for the very wealthy. A nobleman would own an estate and hunt his own deer, and fish in his own streams. Anyone who trespassed on his land to hunt or fish was a poacher and might be imprisoned or even hanged. In fact, when they first met local Native American tribes, colonists thought the women were very hardworking because they farmed, while the men were lazy aristocrats because they hunted and fished all day.

Desperate Times

Although surrounded by food, the settlers began to starve to death. The years 1609 and 1610 were known as the "Starving Time." Of the 214 original Jamestown colonists, only 60 survived. They slaughtered their horses first, then dogs, cats, and rats. They boiled the leather of their shoes. There is even evidence that the survivors resorted to **cannibalism**—or the consumption of human flesh— to stay alive. Human bones recovered from the site show signs of butchering.

An English supply ship finally provided relief. Eventually, the colonists learned to use the abundant natural resources. Relations with the local Native American tribes, such as the Powhatan Confederacy, and the Wampanoag, were sometimes good, sometimes bad. But it was from the Native Americans that the colonists learned how to survive.

New Foods

The New World was full of new fruits, vegetables, and grains. Among the foods found in the colonies but not in Europe were corn (**maize**), wild rice, peanuts, sunflowers, blueberries, pawpaws, pecans, walnuts, chestnuts, maple syrup, and many kinds of squashes and beans. Some other foods found in Central or South America and later introduced to the English colonies and Europe included peppers, tomatoes, and potatoes.

The colonists, initially, weren't impressed by the Native American farms. To them, the fields seemed jumbled and disorganized. The English were used to huge fields with neat, ordered rows. The Native American fields had lumps and mounds, and different kinds of produce were all grown together.

Three Sisters

Most of the tribes the colonists encountered used the "**Three Sisters**" method of agriculture. For each planting they would make a flat-topped mound. Five kernels of corn would be planted in the center of the mound—*one for the blackbird, one for the crow, one for the cutworm, and two to grow.* Climbing beans would be later planted at the base of the corn. They would use the corn stalk for support. Squashes such as pumpkins with vines that spread along the ground would be planted among the mounds. They would serve as living mulch to keep weed growth under control. The farmers would bury a small fish, such as a menhaden, in the mound to act as fertilizer.

The Native American tribes planted with the "Three Sisters" method, mixing corn, squash, and beans in the same plots.

Later, the colonists brought crops from England, such as turnips, cabbages, onions, peas, and carrots. They also grew apples, which provided fruit, and more importantly, **cider**. Water was often contaminated, so alcoholic drinks such as beer and hard apple cider were safer to drink. Even children drank beer and cider, though it was usually much weaker than today. Only about 1 percent alcohol content was needed to kill most harmful microbes.

Livestock

Colonists learned to hunt local animals such as deer, turkeys, geese, and rabbits. They also learned to fish, and to gather shellfish such as oysters. It wasn't long before livestock were imported. Cattle were kept in fenced pastures and provided milk and meat. Pigs often ran wild. They would be branded with distinctive cuts on the ears and turned loose in the woods to feed on acorns. Later, they would be rounded up and claimed by their owners. Sometimes hogs were released on small islands to run free.

Beef was the preferred meat, but beef supplies often ran low by late winter or early spring. Pigs, however, were always plentiful, and their meat could be easily cured. Their meat was smoked for hams or barrel cured with salt.

Though beef was the colonists' favorite meat, pigs were more plentiful, so ham and salt pork became staples of their diet.

Many of the earliest settlers had to learn how to cook from scratch. Even those who had some notion of cooking found some of the new foods to be very strange. The mussels, oysters, and lobsters the Native Americans ate repulsed them. For a long time, both the British and the North American colonists thought the tomato was poisonous. Corn was long considered only fit for animal

Lowly Corn

Corn, or maize, was originally considered only suitable for animal feed. In fact, the first suggestion that the colonists embrace corn would have likened to someone today encouraging people to eat dog food. Eventually, though, colonists and the British came to appreciate corn's taste and nutrition.

Founding father and inventor Benjamin Franklin was a big advocate of corn. He called it "one of the most agreeable and wholesome grains in the world." Today, we mostly eat green corn, when the kernels are soft. Colonists enjoyed it that way when it was in season, but they mostly dried the corn and ground it into a meal. Franklin also learned the Native American technique of making popcorn.

feed. Eventually, though, they adapted, and most of the new foods were accepted. After a while, food in the American colonies was similar to that in England. With an abundance of foodstuffs and colonists with more refined palates, there was a market for professional cooks.

TWO

Becoming a Cook

Visitors to such historical reenactment sites as Historical Williamsburg are sometimes surprised to find all kinds of people cooking. Not only do the reenactors portraying servants and **slaves** work in the kitchen, so does the lady of the house, and often even the men and the children. By the 1700s, most people in colonial America knew how to cook, at least a little.

Still, in most families the women and the female servants or slaves did most of the cooking. The majority of cooks were not professionally trained. The most common way to become a cook was to be trained by one's mother. Techniques and recipes were passed down from generation to generation. As new foods and new procedures became popular, these were added to the general store of knowledge.

Whether rich or poor, the main job of most colonial women was to take care of the home.

Except in the richest households, the housewife was in charge of all household affairs. (The richest could have a staff of servants and slaves, and leave the management of the house to a trained housekeeper, maids, footmen, and a professional cook.) Taking care of the home was considered to be a woman's proper profession. Very few had jobs outside of the home. They would either do all of the cooking themselves, or, if they could afford a servant or two, supervise their labor or work alongside them.

Cookbooks

Besides word of mouth and knowledge passed from mother to daughter, some people learned to cook from cookbooks. There weren't a great many to choose from. Initially, all of these books were imported from England. *The Compleat Housewife*, or *Accomplish'd Gentlewoman's Companion* by Eliza Smith was first published in London in 1727, and later in the colonies in 1742. It contained many recipes, as well as household cleaning hints and remedies for several common diseases.

The most popular cookbook at the time in both England and America was Hannah Glasse's *The Art of Cookery made Plain and Easy*. She wrote it with servants in mind, and her writing style was friendly and easy to understand. Many of her recipes remain popular today in England, such as Yorkshire pudding and gooseberry fool.

These cookbook writers, as well as hundreds of professional female cooks, were challenging the idea that only a man could be a master chef. The old way of thinking was that women could be good household cooks, but only men could be truly skilled artisans in the kitchen.

Apprenticeship

Those who didn't have a mother to pass down knowledge might **apprentice** themselves to a professional cook. In colonial America, most young people who wanted to learn a skill or craft would bind themselves to a teacher, or master in that craft, for a fixed period of years. They would sign a contract promising to work without pay, and learn everything the master had to teach them. Afterward, they had the skill and experience to work for themselves.

Often, a cook's apprenticeship was informal. A girl would be hired as a servant, and she might help out in all aspects of household care—cooking, sewing, cleaning, and minding children. Later, if she had a particular interest or skill in cooking, she might specialize in that.

The Humble Kitchen Maid

Sometimes a maid would be hired specifically to work in the kitchen. She would begin her service as a kitchen maid, under-cook, or assistant cook. She would wake up before anyone in the household and light or stoke the cooking fire. She would also be responsible for the harder or more tedious work, such as scouring pots with sand to clean them, or peeling and chopping vegetables. Gradually, as her work improved, she would be assigned more complex tasks.

Often, the cook or assistant cook would be an **indentured servant**. These women, facing grim prospects at home in England or Ireland, signed their freedom away for up to seven years in exchange for passage to the colonies and the chance at a new life. They had

A kitchen maid was in charge of the hardest (and often the most boring) labor until she learned the art of fine cooking.

to serve whoever sponsored them, and had only a few more rights than slaves. Their master or mistress could beat them. If they ran away, they could be hunted down. But many learned a valuable skill in the New World. When the term of their indenture was up, they were free to work as professional cooks and often did very well.

A Good Career

Becoming a skilled cook was a path to independence for a woman. She could work at a tavern or inn, set up her own restaurant, or work

A well-trained cook might find success working in one of the popular taverns.

The First American Cookbook

One of the most interesting cookbook writers was Amelia Simmons. She described herself as an "American Orphan" who, without any family or connections, was forced to enter domestic service. She worked hard and learned every trick of the kitchen. Though she was just barely literate, she wanted to share her knowledge of cooking. Amelia Simmons became the first person, male or female, to write and publish a cookbook in America. Her *American Cookery* was published in 1796.

She was one of the first to use American foods in her cookbook. Previous books only mentioned English ingredients, some of which were hard to get in the colonies. She helped popularize the words "cookie" and "slaw" and used typically American ingredients such as pumpkins and cranberries.

in a private household. If she chose the latter, she was at or near the top of the servant hierarchy. When she wasn't making meals she had a little free time to herself. She could also supplement her income by selling scraps, fat for soap or candle making, and might even be paid by local butchers and grocers to patronize their shop over their competitors'.

THREE

The Cook's Day

Meals during colonial times were on a somewhat different schedule than they are today. Both the timing and the contents of the meal depended on a person's status and wealth.

Breakfast was usually a light meal, consisting of bread and milk, or **porridge** made of grains that had simmered by the fire overnight. They might also have a glass of beer or cider. The poor tended to eat breakfast around five or six o'clock because they had to begin work very early. Wealthy people woke later, and ate later, perhaps around eight or nine o'clock. Their breakfasts were often just as simple, though they might add a little fish or meat.

Whether the cook was the housewife or a hired servant, she had to get out of bed at about five in the morning to start work. First, she tended to the fire. The hearth used for cooking could be huge, measuring up to 10 feet (3 meters) wide. The fire wasn't usually allowed to cease burning entirely—the cook would rekindle it from the glowing coals. She would draw water and begin to heat it, and also heat the Dutch oven, a heavy cast-iron pot. If she had an assistant, the cook might be able to sleep an hour later and let her helper do these first tasks.

Baking Day

Though some cooks bought bread from a bakery, many made their bread at home.

The fireplace or hearth was the center of kitchen life, and the flames were rarely allowed to go completely out.

Bread was baked in a separate brick oven. The process was so time consuming that many cooks devoted an entire day each week to baking. On baking day, the family ate lightly, eating premade pies or cold meat.

All of the dough would be made and kneaded early in the morning, and then left to rise while the oven heated to the proper temperature. A wood fire was lit, and allowed to burn for up to five hours until

A baker relied on experience to heat an oven to just the right temperature for a perfect loaf of bread.

only ashes remained. The brick walls of the oven held enough heat to do the baking.

After raking the coals and ashes out, the cook then tested the temperature. Because there were no thermometers, the cook stuck her arm inside and guessed, based on her experience, whether the oven was hot enough. One common method involved pain tolerance. If she had to pull her arm out by the count of five, the oven was too hot. If she could stand to leave her arm in the oven for fifteen seconds, it was too cold.

Small loaves and buns could be baked directly on the bricks. Larger loaves and cakes were placed on baking pans. Heavy, dense breads were put in the back of the oven, while lighter cakes that would be taken out first were placed toward the front. Once baked, they were removed with a large shovel-like utensil called a **peel**.

Planning the Meals

If it was not a baking day, a cook in a prosperous household would send breakfast to the family in the dining room. Servants were fed in the kitchen. After breakfast, she would usually consult with the lady of the house about the day's (or week's) menu.

Sometimes the cook's mistress took a very active role in meal preparation. Most of the wealthiest women probably did not don aprons, push up their sleeves, and actually help their cook. They did, however, consult about the menus and offer advice on purchasing and preparing. A highly trained cook might have hated the interference. However, the mistress might serve a valuable purpose if the cook was illiterate, as so many servants and slaves were. The lady of the house could read aloud from one of the popular cookbooks so the cook could learn new recipes.

Visiting the Market

The cook often visited the market on particular days after breakfast was finished. Perhaps two days a week she would go out with her basket over her arm and pick out the best vegetables, fruits, meats, sugar, tea, and spices. Other items, such as milk and eggs, might be delivered. She might make special trips for items that easily spoiled, such as fish.

Butchers, bakers, and grocers would compete to be her favorite provider. Her mistress might give her a strict **budget** for the week, so she would haggle for the best prices. Some vendors would try to trick her into buying low-quality foods. Old fish would be splashed with water to look fresher, or might even have their gills painted, or dabbed with blood, to make them look as if they had just been caught. Bad cheese would be covered with saltpeter. Milk would be warmed by a fire and then sold as "fresh from the cow." The cook had to be on her guard.

Dinner: The Midday Meal

In colonial America, there was no meal called lunch. Dinner was served at midday. It was the largest meal of the day. The poor generally ate dinner at around noon. They had been laboring since sunup, and were eager to have something hot and sustaining after their quick breakfast of bread or porridge. The cook in a poor household might serve a stew with pork, cabbage, and other vegetables, as well as bread. People ate from **trenchers**, or elongated dishes made of wood or metal. Sometimes they used stale bread as a bowl. After they finished their stew, they might eat the softened bread, feed it to the pigs, or give it to someone even poorer.

A Basic Dinner

A cook to a more prosperous farming family would probably serve one or two kinds of meat for dinner. Beef was the favorite, with pork, lamb or **mutton**, and **game** following. Today, puddings and pies are usually sweet and served for dessert. In colonial America, cooks made savory pies and puddings from meat, fruit, and spices. There might be a side dish of vegetables, and pickles were common. In a less-wealthy household, the cook (who might also be the wife and mother of the household) would often serve the food herself.

An Elaborate Dinner

The upper classes usually ate dinner somewhat later, in the midafternoon, around two o'clock. This was a social time, and the family would linger over dinner for a long while. Friends were often invited, and conversation was encouraged.

For those who could afford it, dinner was a very heavy meal. The cook often used many kinds of meats. The first course of a typical dinner in an upper-class household might include soup, such as a spicy watercress soup. It might also include Virginia ham, a roast of beef or lamb, and a chicken, goose, or turkey. Smaller animals such as ducks or young **suckling pigs** might be served with their heads on. The first course might also have vegetables such as potatoes or parsnips, and also heavy, spicy cakes. All of the dishes were put on the table at once.

The second course was usually slightly lighter than the first. The cook might prepare fish, a fricassee of rabbit, fried ox tongue, a casserole of beef with onions or other vegetables, and a salad. Vegetables such as green beans or spinach might be served in a butter and flour sauce similar to a modern béchamel.

A cook preparing formal dinner in a wealthy household could make as many as twenty-five separate dishes.

One popular dish that a cook might be called on to prepare for upper-class colonists was oyster ice cream. This was a savory dish, not a dessert, and would have been served during the second course. It had the taste of a rich and flavorful frozen chowder. Other dishes made into ice cream and served with dinner include asparagus, cheese, and chestnuts.

Dessert

When the cook made desserts, she had to make sure they were light. No one would have room for much more food. Candied rinds of lemons and oranges were popular, as were sugared nuts and tiny figures made of marzipan, or almonds ground up with sugar. For a special treat, the cook might make a **syllabub**, a dessert made from whipped cream, wine or liquor, sugar, spices, and sometimes fruit.

The cook in a prosperous household might have to prepare up to twenty-five different dishes for a fancy dinner, and between five and ten dishes for everyday

After a big dinner, the cook and her assistants still had to clean up the pots and dishes.

meals. She probably had several assistants to help her. The diners usually did not sample each and every dish, but only helped themselves to a few of their favorites. In the wealthiest houses, all of the utensils and table linens were cleared and replaced between courses.

A Light Supper

Supper was a much lighter meal. Served around eight o'clock, it was almost more of a bedtime snack. It might be very similar to breakfast, so the cook would have to do no more than serve bread, porridge, and ale. Or it could be leftovers from the midday dinner.

The colonial American cooks didn't have refrigeration (though occasionally, wealthy people might have a supply of ice for part of the year). Most food had to be eaten quite soon after it was prepared or it would spoil. So any leftovers were eaten either for supper or the next day's breakfast, or they were given to the servants or slaves.

The Danger of Burns

Cooking could be a hazardous occupation. Most cooking was done over or near an open fire. Experienced cooks knew to wear wool or a linen and wool blend called linsey-woolsey, because cotton clothes caught fire so easily. Little children, who often wore cotton, could be badly burned if they got too near the hearth.

The Turnspit Dog

The most common way to cook meat in colonial America was to roast it on a spit over a fire. The meat had to be constantly turned so it would cook evenly and not burn. In earlier times, a person—usually a child or servant—had to perform this tedious task. Later, a contraption allowed a small dog running on a wheel to turn the spit.

Called turnspit dogs, these canines had long bodies and short legs. They usually worked in teams of two, one taking over when the other tired. Though there are stories of the dogs being beaten or having hot coals applied to their feet to make them run, others were treated as pets. When they weren't working in the kitchen, they were used as foot warmers.

Later, mechanical jacks run by heat or steam replaced the dogs. Turnspit dogs are extinct today, but they probably resembled the breed known as a corgi.

The turnspit dog made sure roasts were evenly cooked over a fire.

Despite precautions, burns were common among cooks. One healer reported that many women burned their feet and ankles because liquid would slop out of the pot when they pulled it from the fire and set it on the floor. Burns on the arms and neck were also common. Many female slaves (who might cook for their masters or for their own families in their quarters) were often identified by the burns they had from cooking fires and splashing grease.

Other Duties

In addition to preparing meals, the cook might also have to tend a vegetable and herb garden, pickle and preserve fruits and vegetables, brew beer or cider, or make cheese and butter. Since food couldn't be refrigerated or frozen, a cook or housewife had to spend almost as much time preserving food for future use as she did cooking it. Though she had very busy days, an efficient cook could often steal an hour or so of rest between meals. She rarely had a day off.

Still, it was one of the best jobs in domestic service. A good cook was an artist, and was usually appreciated as such. People rarely thanked maids for making their beds or scrubbing their floors. However, a cook who prepared a delicious meal would often be thanked, and might even be called into the dining room so all of the guests could express their enjoyment of her cooking.

FOUR

The Cook in the Community

Unlike today, all food in colonial America was seasonal. People ate fresh apples in the fall, green salads in the spring, ripe corn in the summer. A cook had to tailor her menu to fit the foods that were available. Or, she had to adapt recipes to use preserved foods in their various forms. The cook probably had a kitchen garden, where she grew herbs and some vegetables. But in a town at least, she relied on farmers and grocers to provide fresh produce. She knew the growing schedules so she could plan her meals ahead of time to use whatever would be ripening.

The Butcher

Though some rural families would slaughter their own livestock, most people in towns relied on the butcher to supply their meat.

The person who raised the cows, pigs, or sheep would drive them to a place near the town, then the butcher would kill them and cut them into pieces for sale. He would usually use an ax both for the slaughter, and to cut the animal up. Most cuts of meat were much larger than they are today.

If a pig was killed in the summer, it was usually eaten right away, because pork spoils very quickly. Sometimes a farm cook would do her own slaughtering. When a farm pig was killed in the hot weather, neighbors would

Pork was salted and then hung in a smokehouse. The smoke gave the meat extra flavor.

be invited over to eat every last bit. When a hog was killed in the winter, it was usually preserved and made into hams.

The butcher used salt to preserve beef and pork. Shoulders, hams, and bacon cuts of pork were layered with salt mixed with brown sugar and saltpeter and left in tubs for about eight weeks. When the salt had removed all the extra moisture, the pork was covered in wood ash to keep bugs away and hung in the smokehouse. The smoke didn't preserve the meat, but it added color and flavor.

Beef, which was harder to preserve because it held more moisture, needed an extra step. After it was dry salted, it was packed in brine, or very salty water, and stored in barrels. The salted meat could last for several years. Hams might be eaten as they were, but salted beef was soaked in water for a long time to remove the excess salt.

The Baker

Some cooks did their own baking, but since this was such a time-consuming process, many relied on a baker. Wheat (often imported from England) was ground into flour by a miller. The baker used this flour to make breads, buns, and cakes. Bakers also made specialty breads such as gingerbread, and might also hire out their ovens for baking meat pies. Warm and fragrant, bakeries were a favorite place for cooks and housewives to meet and linger, especially on cold or wet days.

The Brewer

Since various kinds of alcohol were the most commonly consumed beverages (followed by tea before the Revolution, and coffee afterward) the colonial cook had to visit the brewer or distiller to supply her household's drinking needs. Beer was made with malted grains such as wheat, and hops for flavor. Hard apple cider was made with small,

Few people drank water because it was often contaminated. However, even small amounts of alcohol killed most bacteria, so most people drank beer or cider.

very tart apples. These were both fermented with yeast. When the yeast consumes starches such as grains and fruit, it gives off alcohol. Stronger spirits such as rum were distilled to concentrate the alcohol.

The Smiths

Cooks relied on other members of the community to practice their trade. Many of the cook's tools were made out of iron by a blacksmith. The heavy pots and Dutch ovens were iron, as were pokers for the fire, spoons, knives, ladles, and tongs. The spit, whether a simple turning rod or a mechanical spit jack, was also made of iron. Copper or copper-lined pans were made by the coppersmith, who was also known as a redsmith. He might also make fancy, decorative molds for cakes, jellies, and aspics. The pewtersmith or tinsmith—also known as a whitesmith—might make dishes and cups. Fancier households might have silverware made by a silversmith. (China dishes were mostly made abroad and imported.)

The Woodsmen

The cook also relied on woodsmen for the vast amounts of wood she needed to keep her cooking fire going. Oak was a favored wood, but other woods such as hickory were also used. The colonies were near vast forests that kept the fireplaces well stocked—at least in the beginning. Later, wood became scarcer, especially near big cities. Many utensils were also made of wood, including spoons and the peel, the tool used to remove bread from an oven.

The Rich

Above all, a highly trained cook depended on the wealthy. When the rich settled in towns such as Philadelphia or Boston, they established a social life that demanded frequent entertaining. To show off their wealth, they needed an excellent cook. Once someone had a reputation as a good cook, there could be stiff competition for his or her services. Some wealthy families would try to steal another family's cook. They might tempt her with higher pay, a liberal budget, or days off. Though cooks rarely became wealthy themselves, many were able to save for a comfortable retirement, or perhaps opened a tavern or restaurant of their own.

FIVE

The Colonial Cook's Legacy

Today, the United States is home to very diverse cuisine, with roots in English food, special American additions, and frequent borrowings from around the world. Still, some of the regional specialties that began in colonial times are considered typical of certain parts of the United States.

The English settlers came to the colonies in four main waves of immigration. Also, settlers from other countries tended to live in particular areas, so cooks shared knowledge and melded their cooking traditions. Their traditions live on in these regions today.

The Puritan Legacy

The Puritans settled in New England. They didn't believe in too much pleasure, and saw eating as simply something necessary to

The Puritans introduced an American favorite: apple pie.

survive. Their food tended to be simple and plain. Baked beans and dark bread are still popular in the area. The Puritans also baked frequently, and such American staples as apple pie and turkey baked in an oven (as opposed to spit-roasted) began in New England. They also made boiled stews of meat mixed with vegetables. In other regions, the meat and vegetables were usually cooked separately.

Only later did cooks begin to take advantage of the abundant seafood found in the region. Today places such as Boston are known for lobster dishes and seafood chowders.

The Chesapeake Influence

The next group of immigrants, arriving in Virginia and the Chesapeake area during the mid-seventeenth century, were a combination of Cavaliers, or the English noblemen who supported the king in the English Civil War, and poor peasants from the south of England. The noblemen continued their preference for a lavish lifestyle, and favored beef and game. Roast beef was a particular favorite.

The poor, including free white people and

Immigrants who settled in the Chesapeake region gave America traditional southern foods like cornbread, greens, and fried chicken.

black slaves, ate much more humble food. Mixing English, colonial, and African traditions, they developed what is today known as typical Southern food. Cornbread, greens cooked with salt pork, and fried chicken were staples. These dishes continue to be prepared by many Southern cooks.

The Quaker Contributions

The mostly Quaker colonists who arrived in the mid-Atlantic and Delaware Valley region in the seventeenth century came originally from the north of England. They were similar to Puritans in their desire for simplicity. A cook in that region would boil many of her dishes. Boiled apple dumplings were served almost every day in many households, and other kinds of boiled puddings and dumplings were popular. Two favorites that originated there, and are still popular today, are apple butter and cream cheese.

German immigrants joined the Quakers in the area in the mid-eighteenth century, and introduced one of the most famous regional dishes: **scrapple**. Leftover pork or pig offal (liver, heart, and other organs) was minced and mixed with cornmeal and spices, formed into a loaf, sliced, and fried. Scrapple is still frequently served in the area.

Revolutionary Coffee

Why do the English drink tea, while most Americans favor coffee? The Tea Act of 1773 was an effort by the British to force the colonists to pay tax on imported teas. The colonists strongly objected. This led to the Boston Tea Party, where a group of colonists boarded a British ship and dumped the tea overboard. It also increased conflicts that eventually led to the America Revolutionary War that began in 1775.

Patriots said that to resist the British and show their spirit, colonists should give up tea and turn instead to coffee. Housewives refused to serve tea, and it wasn't long before coffee became America's drink of choice.

Irish and Scottish Flavor

The last wave came in the mid to late eighteenth century and settled into what is known as the backcountry. These people were of Irish and Scottish descent, and unlike many in the three other waves of immigration, were mostly from poor backgrounds. They often came to the colonies fleeing famines. They brought their cuisines with them, though they had to make some substitutions. They couldn't get oats for their usual mush, so they substituted corn, making the

Irish and Scottish immigrants couldn't always get the oats they loved, so they substituted corn, popularizing the grits that are still eaten in the South today.

popular Southern dish, grits. They introduced potatoes to the region, as well as a soured milk dish called **clabber**, which survives today in a similar form in buttermilk and yogurt.

Today, the United States is part of the global market, and its cuisines can contain elements from around the world. But the cooks of the thirteen colonies had a profound influence on typical American food, and their innovations can still be seen today.

Glossary

apprentice   A person bound to learn a trade from a master for a fixed period of years, usually with little or no pay.

budget   An amount of money allowed for a certain time or a particular purpose.

cannibalism   Eating the flesh of other humans; generally, an animal eating the flesh of its own kind.

cider   A drink, which may be either fermented (alcoholic) or unfermented (nonalcoholic), made from fruit, mainly apples.

clabber   A drink or food made from soured, clotted milk.

colonist   A person who settles in a colony separate from their native country; specifically, British settlers who came to America in the seventeenth and eighteenth centuries.

entrepreneur   A person who takes risks to start a business or enterprise.

game   Animals that are hunted for food or sport.

hardtack   A mix of flour and water baked very dry and hard; generally used as provisions on ships.

indentured servant   A person who is contracted to labor for another person for a fixed period, often without pay but frequently in exchange for passage to another country.

maize   The word used by the British for the crop known today as corn; in colonial times, in Britain, "corn" was used for all grain crops, such as wheat or rye.

mutton   The meat of a mature sheep (as opposed to lamb, the meat of a young sheep).

peel   A shovel-like instrument used by bakers for moving bread into and out of an oven.

porridge
: A dish made of grains such as oats, wheat, or corn boiled in water or milk.

scrapple
: A dish of meat scraps mixed with cornmeal made into a loaf, sliced, and fried.

slave
: A person who is the property of another person and has no individual rights.

suckling pig
: A young pig that is still nursing, often roasted whole.

syllabub
: A dessert, drink, or fortifying food made of cream flavored with wine or spirits, and often spices and sugar.

Three Sisters
: A method of farming in which corn, squash, and beans are grown together, usually on mounds.

trencher
: A plate or platter for food, often made of wood but sometimes made of metal.

turnspit dog
: A small dog with short legs that runs inside a wheel that turns meat roasting on a spit over a fire.

Find Out More

BOOKS

Ichord, Loretta Frances. *Hasty Pudding, Johnnycakes, and Other Good Stuff: Cooking in Colonial America*. Minneapolis, MN: Millbrook Press, 1998.

Raum, Elizabeth. *The Dreadful, Smelly Colonies: The Disgusting Details About Life in Colonial America*. Minneapolis, MN: Capstone Press, 2011.

Simmons, Amelia. *The First American Cookbook: A Facsimile of "American Cookery," 1796*. New York: Oxford University Press, 1958.

WEBSITES

Kid Info

www.kidinfo.com/american_history/colonization_colonial_life.html

This section on life in colonial America has many topics to choose from, including several articles on colonial food and cooking.

US History

www.ushistory.org/us/index.asp

Find out all about the history of the place now known as the United States, from pre-Columbian times to today.

MUSEUMS

Colonial Williamsburg

www.history.org/history/museums

This living history museum in Williamsburg, Virginia, recreates an entire colonial city. The 301-acre (122-hectare) site has many original historic buildings, and actors/docents who reenact colonial life, including cooks working in homes and in taverns, bakers, brewers, butchers, and more. The website is also full of valuable information about the era.

The Culinary Arts Museum

www.culinary.org

Located at Johnson and Wales University in Providence, Rhode Island, this museum has many exhibits that focus on food history and other aspects of food and cooking.